F'D UP MY CREDIT

How To Navigate and Find The Advantages In
A Disadvantaged Credit Reporting System For
Black America

JEREMI'E G. ROBERTS

Disclaimer:

This book is a collective combination of my life's experiences and real life events that I've endured, witnessed, or have researched. By no means am I giving any legal or tax advice. Please consult with a licensed professional for any of those needed services.

Publishing by Zjae Productions

For more information on special discounts for bulk purchases, please contact Zjae Productions by mail, email or phone.

Zjae Productions
P.O. Box 924
Aylett, VA 23009

Email: zjae13@aol.com

Phone: 804-885-0558

I want to dedicate this book...

To my mother, Margaret Roberts (deceased), who
was a dedicated educator for many years:
You were a true example of sacrifice to me,
with all that you gave up to provide for our
family. I'm the man I am today because of
you.

To my beautiful wife Stacey W. Roberts, who has
stuck with me through so many losses:
My best friend, my love, my heart, my
balancer I've learned so much from you and
pray that GOD will continue to use you as a
vessel.

To my six children, Kiara, Kaleb, Cayla, Caylan
(deceased), Cori, and Clarke:
Each one of you have shown me the real

meaning of GOD's mercy, grace, and favor. I don't deserve such blessings and I'm eternally grateful. I pray that you're proud of your dad and you'll never doubt my love for you.

FOREWORD

Dr. Michael Jones-Richmond City Councilman/Senior

Pastor Village Of Faith

So much is written today to inspire and encourage us. It is necessary, however, we need to get fired up about our financial houses. How do we get practical information to people that is "digestible" and relatable? F'd Up My Credit grabs your attention and Jeremi'e doesn't let go. Hold on for a financial ride that can get you back on track. Divorce, bankruptcy and just bad decisions get so many of us off course and we need a basic approach to get us back on task. Take the necessary steps to take control of your financial life by seeing that life doesn't end at the loss of a six figure salary. If your credit is messed up, you are in the right place.

INTRODUCTION

"Sir, please keep your seatbelt fastened until we stop at the gate."

Here I sit. Impatiently I wait to exit the plane that has just touched down in my hometown of Houston, Texas, so I can get to my mother who is in the hospital. The plane finally comes to a complete stop but for some reason it seems like it's going to take forever to exit. I watch as the people stand around slowly retrieving their bags from the overhead compartment.

"Sir, are you ok?" asks the flight attendant.

"Yes, Ma'am. I just want to get off of here, pick up my rental, and head to the hospital to be with my momma." All I could think of was my mother's diagnosis of stage four cancer and the uncertainty of her life expectancy at this point. I just wanted to see her.

"Sir, I hope and pray that she'll be okay," she says, "Oh, look, the line is moving. Things are looking better already."

I exit the plane, retrieve my bags and immediately take the shuttle to the car rental area. This is where stuff gets real.

As I approach the counter with my bags in one hand and debit card and driver's license in the other, the rental car associate greets me with a smile.

"Good morning, sir. Do you have a reservation?"

"Yes, I do. It's under last name, Roberts first name, Jeremi'e," I reply.

"Okay. There you are and it looks like you've paid already. I'll just need your I.D. and major credit card," she says.

"Sure. Here you go."

"Are you here on business or visiting family?" she asks.

"Oh, no Ma'am. My mom is in the hospital and I'm going to see her," I reply.

"You seem like a good son. Oh, Mr. Roberts, this is a debit card. We'll need a major credit card on file."

"I don't have a credit card. All I have is my debit card. Plus, I've already paid for the rental," I plea.

"Mr. Roberts, we only accept major credit cards when you pick up the rental," she replies.   I begin to get a little frustrated because I want to be with my mom. I had already paid for the rental online through one of those bidding sites. So, I leave the counter and walk up to several other counters that would only accept major credit cards as well. I feel so defeated.

I remember that I do have a major credit card with me but, it's a corporate card from the company I work for and is only to be used for company travel. Now, violating that rule could bring about disciplinary actions up to termination. I'm the only one employed because my wife is a stay-at-home mom, so I will be risking a lot if I use this card.

Suddenly, I see a sign at another counter that states they accept debit cards with a two hundred dollar deposit. I have about one hundred dollars over that amount in my account so I figure I can make this work. *Just get me to my Momma,* I think.

I approach the counter with a tired look of defeat,

yet am hopeful. The gentleman there greets me. "Hello, sir. How may I help you today?" he asks.

I begin to explain to him what I've been through and how I'm trying to get to my mom. He kindly takes my card and identification and assures me that he will find me the best rates after he pulls my credit.

"What? Wait, what do you mean you have to pull my credit?" I ask.

"Yes, sir. Whenever someone pays using a debit card we have to do a small credit check," he replies.

"Okay. Whatever." I say.

He taps on a few keys, there is a brief pause and then his facial expression goes from a smile to a person struggling with gas pains in the middle of a prayer service. "I'm sorry, Mr. Roberts. But, we wouldn't be able to rent you a vehicle using a debit card based upon our system after the credit pull. I am so sorry."

I sadly reflect on how in my mid thirty's, I feel like a failure in just about every area of my life. I have gone from a six-figure income by the time I was thirty, owning a business, a Mercedes, a Porsche, a house, having savings accounts, 401K, a few others things that I eventually lost, to this. I stand here with these bags in my hand, with no way to go see my mom and it is killing me softly. I have a decision to make.

I can spend a good portion of the only money I have in my account to catch a cab, try to call someone to come and pick me up with such short notice or use this corporate card knowing that there will eventually be consequences. I feel like a lost child and am embarrassed to look any of these rental associates in the eye.

I sit down for a while and watch other people there to pick up their rental cars, gladly pull out their purses and wallets with their major credit cards and with a smile. Tears begin to well up in my eyes as I think about this failure of a son my mother has, who can't even get to her when she is in the hospital.

I reach into my wallet and pull out that corporate card. *They just need a card on file. It's not like they're not gonna release the hold after I return the car.*

WAIT. Are you judging me? What would you have done?

You know, when I returned to the first counter I visited when I first arrived, I briefly imagined something that could have been the answer to my distress. I imagined that I had "FIXED UP MY CREDIT." This entire experience cut deep and made me more aware of the importance of having good credit. Credit is like a combination to a safe or a bank vault full of money and opportunities. Why didn't I know this sooner? Why don't they teach this stuff in schools?

I share this story with you because certain scenes in life can seem like it's the end to a horrible, sad film but one small portion of a movie isn't the full and complete motion picture. I also want to show how a series of life's events will either push or pull you depending on your perspective and how well equipped you are or are not.

I believe for many blacks here in America we started the race in a deficit and due to the lack of knowledge, in particular when it comes to credit rating, we are at a huge disadvantage. There is much work to do if we are to obtain financial freedom or to be financially independent. This book is purposed to inform, inspire, encourage, equip, touch, uplift, and teach you about the value of a great credit rating.

I don't want to fail to mention that this book may make you cry, get angry, frustrated, fed up, and even down right mad with a system that was designed to derail black America from truly becoming equal on an economic level as other ethnicities, mainly white America. Dr. Martin Luther King Jr. said, "It's a cruel jest to tell a bootless man that he ought to pull himself up by his own bootstraps."

By the way, this book may cause me to lose my job.

I see and analyze people's credit everyday to see if they are homebuyer-worthy or not, initially based off of their credit scores. I must admit that we'll be going into some rough turbulence and some strong winds, so please keep your seat belts fastened until we arrive at the gate of our destination.

Chapter 1

DON'T BELIEVE THE HYPE

There is an old saying, "You are what you eat." Suggesting that what you take in is what you become, or what you ingest can transform who you are. Many years ago Black America was told that they were free and shared the same rights as all other Americans. Our very own Declaration of Independence even states, "All men are created equal." Yet, today in 2019 blacks continue to fight for justice and equality. So, those of us who digested that, may in fact be living a lie. Many will argue that blacks have the same opportunities as any other ethnic group here in America, however, I believe that the road to those opportunities can be very different.

In order to get a grasp of where we are today as it relates to credit and finances of Black America, we first need to go back to when we were told the lie, that we were free and had equal opportunities. Now, let me assure you that this book is not about promoting hate and anger from one race to another. It's about where we've come from, where we are, and where we're going. That being said, I have to admit that I believe in America today we are indeed living a lie.

In fact, the pressure and tension from the lie grows because in so many ways the cover is being pulled off exposing some naked truths about as some would call it, "the greatest nation in the world." Black people need to understand that our history didn't start with slavery, but, we lived in a land where we were kings and queens with wealth, land, and prosperity. Many of us can research and trace our ancestry roots all the way back to Africa where we had riches and a world system, and structures that still stand today. To be fair with what's talked about in this book, I have to fast forward from us being kings and queens to when we landed in this place called America. I promise you credit scoring and rating will be tied into all of this, but, I have to lay the foundation of the mindset of those that benefited from the blacks that were brought here in the early 1600's and forced into slavery. In addition, we have to take a look at when slavery "ended" and all of the hype surrounding it.

Africans were brought to America for one reason; to generate wealth. Initially, it was all about getting strong abled-bodies to work in the fields, farming and picking tobacco and cotton for free so that these commodities could be sold for huge profits. This way of earning grew fast. More and more blacks were sold into slavery to the benefit of their white slave owners.

Imagine being brought over on a ship where you

constantly witnessed people dying all around you. Not to mention, while on that ship you were shackled and stacked on top of others with a very small, uncomfortable space to lie down. By the way, if you were at the bottom of that stack there were all types of bodily fluids running down on you; urine, feces, menstruation, snot from those that were crying, saliva, vomit from those that were sea sick. You were a stolen people, brought to a stolen land.

Years went by, slave-owners were getting wealthier and America was benefiting by leaps and bounds. They passed the family farming businesses down to their children, who would pass it down to their children, so on and so forth. Generational wealth for whites was on the rise while blacks, who were enslaved, were getting further and further away from who they were and the land that they came from. What does all of this have to do with credit? Well, it's extremely difficult to talk about our present and future without briefly

4

glancing in the rearview mirror at our past; looking at those things that are or should be behind us.

After years of abuse and oppression, black America moved into an era where slavery ended, then into Civil Rights. This was a stage where black people and leaders arose and equality was fought for, and in many cases given; on the surface at least. One of the most instrumental activists during that time was Dr. Martin Luther King, Jr. He dedicated his life to fighting for equality for blacks in America to be able to earn and provide for their families without the fear of being harmed or mistreated. See, during that time in America blacks were still beaten and in many cases killed for speaking out on the unfair treatment they had to endure. He himself was assassinated. I believe it was because of the direction he was leading "America's Most Unwanted".

Dr. King made efforts to expose and demand a stronger financial base from America to the descendants of many of the black slaves whose backs this country's wealth was built upon. He actually began a campaign, "Poor People's Campaign," aimed to assist not just blacks, but poor Americans from different racial backgrounds, by addressing income and housing. In the richest country in the world, people were working yet still finding it difficult to provide a decent living for their families and finding themselves in poverty.

Sadly, right now in 2019, this is still the case for millions of Americans, especially in black communities. In an article written by Mark Engler in 2010 he wrote, "In February 1968, King announced specific demands: $30 billion for antipoverty, full employment, guaranteed income, and the annual construction of 500,000 affordable residences." Dr. King's plan was to bring this campaign to Washington D.C. on May 2, 1968. Some believed that the FBI also followed this effort and made several attempts to interrupt this campaign.

Although the march still took place, it was done without the leadership of Dr. King. He was assassinated on April 4, 1968, one month before this monumental economic equality movement was to take place. Seems that some in power here in the U.S. at the time knew that economic equality would shift the wealth from a small few, to wealth and equality for many, which would have an adverse effect on power and control. I'll refrain from going into too many details on the matter but if you do your own research you'll learn that there may have been plans and conspiracies within our own government to destroy the movement by aiding in the assassination of Dr. King. After many years of fighting for equal rights and blacks in America striving to level the playing fields, several strides were made as it relates to laws and protection acts to promote equality that some of us benefit from today. This is what I call the **HYPE**.

I've worked in the financial industry for over 24 years

and over 15 of those years have been in mortgage lending. I've seen the different laws that have been put in place to protect inequalities and unfair lending acts. Even still being exposed to such information, I still somehow got caught up in the world-wind of damaged credit, exclusion, and victimized of predatory lending. It's one thing having laws in place to protect consumers but it's another thing being enlightened and educated on how we are protected and what we're being protected from. I often make the statement "create the problem and sell the solution" as it relates to an entity creating or being a part of the problem, then making financial from selling the solution.

One example of this, is something that was practiced back in the day called Redlining. Now redlining is illegal and comes with penalties and fines to financial institutions. However, redlining was something that was created, used, and practiced by our government. Now, laws are enforced against it. I would recommend you look into Redlining, Blacklist, National Housing Act of 1934, Federal Housing Administration (FHA), Black-White Wealth Gap, just to name a few. You'll get more background information as it relates to vigorous attempts to maintain and widen the gap between the poor and the rich and between black America and white America through housing and income.

Now, what better way to continue this gap than with something that we know as a credit rating or credit score. "We'd love to give you this loan but, your credit score isn't high enough. Sorry." Please, DON'T BELIEVE THE HYPE!

Chapter 2

LEAVE ME "A LOAN"

I must admit that I was somewhat intimidated when I first got into the business of lending. I remember years ago someone told me that they once earned $10,000 in one month after helping people with their home loans. I was like "Jigga what, Jigga who?" Everything after that part in the conversation wasn't even important to me. All I was doing was spending that $10,000 in my mind.

I retrieved the contact information and decided to call the branch manager for that mortgage office and within a matter of weeks, I was hired. I had no lending background, no understanding of rates or APR, and most definitely no clue regarding credit. As a matter of fact, this company preferred people with little to no experience so that we could learn the business their way. At least that's what they said the reason for that was. I later understood why.

While training to become a loan officer, I got a crash course on there being three main credit bureaus we utilize and how to identify late payments, collections, and charged-off accounts. The main focus was on the credit scores and how that possibly meant more money in my pocket based upon a customer's credit score. The higher their credit score meant there was more of a chance of them getting the loan. On the other hand, if they had a lower credit score, enough to still qualify, then we could justify charging them more cost to do the loan thus more profits and commissions; seemed like a win/win at the time. The customer would get the loan and we would make more money.

I quickly noticed that there was a difference in black people's credit scores and white people's credit scores. There was also a huge difference between the two when it came to credit knowledge and what they were willing to pay for as it relates to the cost of the loan. It was almost as if many of the black customers were just happy that someone wanted to do business with them, so they were willing to take any offer. Lenders took and are still taking advantage of black America like that today.

Later, those of us that had no lending experience learned that it felt like many of the practices condoned and taught by our employer was what we know today as predatory lending. Wikipedia says this about predatory lending: "Predatory lending refers to unethical practices conducted by lending organizations during a loan origination process that are unfair, deceptive, or fraudulent." While there are no legal definitions in the United States for predatory lending per se, a 2006 audit report from the office of the inspector general of the Federal Deposit Insurance Corporation (FDIC) broadly defines predatory lending as "imposing unfair and abusive loan terms on borrowers," however, "unfair" and "abusive" were not specifically defined. Notice how the government allows for a gray area when it comes to this practice and how it's defined?

Credit scores play a very vital role when it comes to getting loans and what type of loans lenders will make available to you. First, let's look at the area where I have spent most of my career; the mortgage industry. When it comes to creating generational wealth and developing financial stability, housing is critical. There are a lot of communities in America where blacks are homeowners but, I often wonder at what cost. Meaning, are we willing to, for the sake of saying that we own our home, pay a much higher interest rate? Are we willing to pay almost double and tripple for that home because of our current credit score and offered rate? I couldn't fail to mention also that the condition of some of the communities are horrible.

Some lenders have specialty loans designed for low-to-moderate income borrowers with lower credit scores and in many cases these loans come with a higher interest rate as opposed to other conventional mortgages. Now ask yourself, what demographics mainly fall into the low-to-moderate income, lower credit score category? I will admit that some of these loan options make it possible for some to become homeowners because of the low down payment requirements and some flexible debt/ratio guidelines, which can be a good thing if the borrower manages it properly.

What I mean by managing the loan properly is when possible, and if the rate is high, refinancing out of that one to a loan with a lower rate. This is possible after getting your credit score up and allows you to avoid paying more in interest over the life of the loan. Also, if you can afford to get a 15-year mortgage instead of a 30-year. You will end up paying less for the home in the long run. Pace yourself and don't bite off more than you can chew.

I know what you may be thinking regarding some of these low-to-moderate income mortgages. You're thinking that this sounds something like the predatory lending practices mentioned earlier in this chapter. Now, do you really think our government would allow something like that to take place with certain lender loopholes? You said it, I didn't.

The next type of loan I want to address are car loans. Have you ever gone to a car dealership and fell in love with a car after test driving it? After that you have to go through the whole loan process and the back and forth with the so-called manager on the pricing and payment amount? You know when you give your sales representative an amount you are willing to pay and they say, "Let me go and speak with my manager." Then, they return from taking a smoke break or talking in the office with another sales rep about the ball game just to tell you that they can only take a small amount off.

So, you complete the application process and after a few hours of being at the dealership you finally get a lender that wants your money, I mean business, just to find out that the payments are higher than what you told the rep you wanted to pay. Whether you take the car or not, you find out very soon that your credit had been ran ten plus times, decreasing your credit score due to all of the inquiries. Now, you are in worse shape than when you first visited the dealership. Your score has dropped and its even more difficult for you to find financing anywhere else. Plus, you don't want to go through that process all over again so you contact that sales representative from the first dealership you went to.

You pick up that new car, with those less than desirable payments, and drive it off the lot all the while with its value decreasing. Oh, let me not fail to mention that 20% interest rate you're paying due to that credit score you now have. I really wish this story was fiction but it isn't. It was something that I experienced and have seen others experience when I worked in the car business for a brief moment. My recommendation is to get your credit score up, then walk into your bank and get a car loan to pay the dealership. It's not worth allowing them to send your information to several different lenders and get all of those inquiries on your credit report.

It sounds a little crazy but, something that simple and seems so normal can have an effect on your credit rating thus leading to paying higher interest rates or even denial. When lenders see that you've applied to several different places by having your credit pulled they will consider you as a risk and maybe hesitate on giving you the loan. The credit-scoring algorithm also subtracts points from your score for credit inquiries. That never made sense to me until just a few years ago. The credit bureaus and even some credit monitoring services will allow creditors to get data on you from what's called a soft pull. Then you'll get something online or in the mail stating that you are pre-approved or that you have a good approval chance for a credit card, car loan, personal loan, etc. You finally apply only to find out that you were declined because of your credit score or something else. Now your credit score has dropped some more all because of that inquiry. So you end up with a lower score and no new credit line, while they've made money from the creditors advertising on their site and then from the actual credit pull. Yeah, just doesn't seem right.

Finally, the last loan type I want to talk about that I have a lot of experience with, not as a lender but as a customer, is the Payday and Title Loan. These are the devil... Okay. They are not the devil but, you can get caught in a cycle where you feel like you've been through hell, so they are close to the devil.

These types of loans have been under heavy scrutiny and in some states don't even exist because of some of their lending practices and the financial burden that can be placed on someone that's already struggling. The times in my life where I've stepped over into the dark side of Payday and Title loans were because I didn't have the credit to get funds from a bank; times when I was in extreme need to get some funds fast. I didn't have enough money to pay rent and other utilities and I found out that all I had to do was show them my current pay-stub, two month's bank statements, ID, and give them my bank account and routing numbers and then they would loan me a percentage of what my regular pay was. No credit needed.

I thought this was the best thing since the light bulb. After all, it didn't matter what the rate was or the terms as long as I could take care of my expenses at the time. My next pay comes around, my direct deposit hits and not too long afterwards my Payday loan repayment hits. Talk about an emotional roller coaster.

Then I remembered that all I had to do was go back up to the place and reapply for the loan to get that money that was subtracted from my account minus a finance charge. I did this pay period after pay period waiting on some more funds over and beyond my check to come in. I then realized that nothing like that was going to happen.

Eventually I paid them off but, ended up doing it again. Finally, the cycle caught up to me and my bank account got overdrawn, eventually closed, ultimately in collections for the Payday loan, and a negative mark with Chex Systems. They are sort of like the credit bureau for bank checking and savings accounts. If you get a bad mark with Chex Systems, then it will become difficult for you to open up another bank account; and if you do you'll get a second chance account that has high monthly service fees.

I finally got in a position to pay our car off but, shortly there after found our finances back in trouble again. I was driving through the Eastside of town and there I see a place that says they will give you money for your car title, up to $2,500. So, I went in just to get some information and before you know it I walked out of there with somewhere around $800, no credit needed. I needed the money and the fact that I only had to pay about $250 back next month and then the following months until it was paid off seemed like a great deal. That was until I made about eight payments and realized I was getting screwed; royally screwed.

I used to be embarrassed to say but, my story may be a blessing to someone. I lost a lot of money and a couple of cars due to Title Loans. They focus on the poor and people with little to no other option and you'll spot them in mostly distressed or black communities. That experience made me realize that I didn't need credit until I needed credit.

My advice to you, based upon my experience, is to avoid Payday and Title loans if at all possible. I have yet to meet someone that built wealth or financially benefited long-term from these kinds of loans except for the owners and the government officials that also own or accept large donations from these companies. Look into that, you'll be amazed by what you find out.

Chapter 3

WHAT YOU DON'T KNOW CAN HURT YOU

Have you ever heard or said, "What you don't know can't hurt you?" Though that statement may sound good, I've found it to be so untrue and misleading. Imagine walking through a minefield not knowing where to step next. Do you think that if you have knowledge of where the mines are that you are less likely to get blown to pieces? Think about that time when your eight-year old daughter was playing with lego pieces in the hallway earlier in the day and you came through that night, and the bottom of your bare feet seemed to find the hardest, sharpest piece ever made. Would knowing that those pieces were down there have saved you some hurt and kept you from shouting that four-letter word? Of course that would be the case. I believe that knowledge is power and used knowledge is even more powerful. Once we learn and understand credit, how it's used, when to use it, and the value of it we'll put ourselves in a position to obtain a better financial state.

About 90% of lenders use the FICO score when deciding to give you a loan or not. This score can range from 300-850. Here is a breakdown on the condition of credit as it relates to the actual credit score. These numbers may vary depending on where you apply but it should give you a general idea:

300-620 Bad

621-680 Fair

681-730 Good

731+ Excellent

This is just an example of how some lenders view your credit score and the type of customer you are based upon your past credit history. It also gives the lender a glimpse of and insight into whether or not you are a risk to them. You will hear lenders say that you are more than just a number. However, you and I both know that it's all about their numbers, the bottom line, and profits. So, the way that they see it, is that the bigger risk you are the more you'll have to pay for it. This is the reason you'll see higher rates and finance charges for those people with lower credit scores.

In some ways I think this is just a cover-up and a way for them to make more money off of the poor and in this case poor black Americans. Knowing what your credit scores mean is great and valuable knowledge to have but you also need to understand what makes that score go up and what areas to focus on when building or rebuilding your credit.

In the diagram below is a chart that shows what makes

up your FICO score. We'll cover some of the meaning behind

each section as well.

What Makes Up Your Fico Score

Payment History- (35%) This is something that's pretty

self-explanatory. It's all about making on-time payments on a

monthly basis. The algorithms take under consideration the

reporting from creditors based upon a payment being 30-,

60-, 90-, or 120-days late. So, there's a bit of a window there

for your payment to be considered late as far as your credit

report is concerned. However, the creditor can enforce a late

fee based upon the agreed upon grace period. So, it is

possible that your payment can be late with the creditor but not late on your credit report.

Credit Utilization- (30%) Pertaining to revolving credit, you'll have a credit limit, credit balance, and available credit. The credit utilization is the ratio between your credit limit and your credit balance. It shows how much credit you have used compared to the credit limit you have. For example, you can have a $1000 credit card limit and use $750 of that credit limit, thus giving you a 75% credit utilization ratio. This is something that hurts a lot of people, especially those that are uneducated when it comes to credit.

Credit History- (15%) Within the algorithm of credit reporting the credit history is another area of importance. This would be how long you've had the credit account by numbers of years. It's important to have more than three years of history due to the fact that 15% of your credit's score is based upon your credit history. Some believe that even bad history can be helpful to that 15%. I'm not saying that, but, I will say to take notice of when you've closed an account or payed off an account like a car or a personal loan. You may see a slight dip in your score because that history will begin to cease. Worry not, your scores will slowly start moving in the right direction.

New Credit- (10%) I have to be really careful with this one. Establishing new credit *can* have an effect on your credit history because it decreases the number of years you have had credit. New credit can also show creditors that other companies want to do business with you, which can give the appearance that you're not a huge risk in some cases.

Types of Credit- (10%) This references having different kinds of credit. For example, credit cards, car loans, home loans, personal loans, etc. The credit scoring system looks for multiple credit type accounts to show that you can manage diversity. I know it can look a little overwhelming in trying to keep up with all of the percentages and paying the bills on time but, you have to remember that it was never designed to be simple and easy. I oftentimes wonder how people who have never worked in the financial industry would be able to understand and keep up with how credit works. After all, even working in the mortgage industry for years I can't say that any one of my peers or managers, for that matter, ever mentioned anything about credit leveraging to create a living or wealth.

I saw and advised people that had wealth of their own regarding home-financing and I saw that something was different with those clients as opposed to the ones that seemed to be living from paycheck-to-paycheck. I noticed the correlation between how they managed money and how they kept their credit and used it for leveraging their buying power. I noticed that the clients with good credit seemed to have a handle or control over their finances. On many occasions I would ask myself why in the world didn't I know this important key to being a financial success.

By the age of 18, I had my first business selling products. Okay, stop what you're thinking. It was legal and legitimate. I sold soap and cleaning products and I had a chance to rub elbows with multi-millionaires and attend learning seminars. I bought the books and listened to the tapes. To this day, I have never heard anyone mention anything about utilizing credit to build and maintain wealth.

I was sold on building a business and getting to a point in life where I could pay cash for a house or a car but, little did I know that maintaining a great credit rating would be and has been the key to obtaining financial freedom. I personally believe that not knowing this sooner hurt me in many ways. You may feel that way also however, I have great news for you. If you're reading this, IT'S NOT TOO LATE!

By buying this book, you have acknowledged that you want to have better, be better, and do better with using your credit to your advantage. Now that you have an idea on how black America was kept out and thrown into a system that wasn't a level playing field, you can make some adjustments to how you play this game. Its like being in a race and everyone is told to take 400 steps forward except you. Then you're told to go, and that everybody is the same and all have the same opportunities to win.

Okay. What do you do now? Do you stop running the race? Do you just give up and point at all of the people that had a head start? NO! What you do is use your GOD given ability to run harder, run faster, and run smarter. You find what's working and duplicate that success principle. You're not tasked with recreating the wheel, you just need to know how to steer it. It's time to reboot our thinking and how we value credit.

I've heard the old folks say back in the day, "What was meant for evil, GOD meant it for my good". (Genesis 50:20) Take control of your credit and do the same.

Chapter 4

CONTROL +ALT +DELETE

One of the most frustrating things is going through life feeling like you aren't living out your purpose and not doing what you were meant to do. I'm on my computer all day long, two or three computers in some cases and my wife will tell you that I'm not the neatest file and document sorter on them. It's not uncommon for me to have one hundred different files directly on my desk top instead of in folders. I'll have seven or eight browsers open at one time with several different apps going too.

No matter how many times it happens, when an app

stops running or gets stuck, or a webpage or video is buffering, I still get frustrated at the computer because it's not doing what I purchased it to do. It's not fulfilling its purpose. Okay, I'm part of the blame but, don't miss my point here. Many times, I'll have to reboot my computer or end a task by pressing at the same time CONTROL+ALT+DELETE.

I'm not going to go into the technical definitions of each term as it relates to computers because I don't know and I don't care. As long as I can get back on the right track with using my computer, that's all that matters to me. I will, however, use CONTROL+ALT+DELETE and put my own meaning to them in this chapter as it relates to us, black America, on how we need to reboot our thinking when it comes to credit.

This book isn't about fixing your credit but, it's about fixing your mindset on how you value it. Don't worry, I'll give you a few tips that I have used and it worked for me with cleaning up my credit. I'm also going to make sure that you have access to several different people, I trust, that specialize in credit-repair. I've seen for myself that they have helped with navigating people from bad credit to great credit. My ultimate goal here is to make sure that your mind is renewed so when you do get that 750 + credit score, you can keep it and use it to your advantage. We have to reboot our thinking, fast, before the game changes again.

CONTROL

Slave owners knew the power that resided in books; thus commanding and demanding slaves, to not read or they could face a beating or even death. Sadly, this inherited pattern of not reading is still within the black community today. One of the best ways to pass on knowledge is through reading and books. If we are to take control over our financial state as black people here in America we have to be willing to invest heavily and expeditiously in learning about credit. It's time to create new habits and develop more of a conscious effort to reinvest in our wealth.

Due to the resources available via the internet, finding out how to build or rebuild your credit is out there. However, there's something that I discovered. People would rather pay someone else to fix their credit instead of getting the knowledge on how the credit system works and how to fix it themselves. I'm not saying that paying someone to assist with fixing your credit is wrong. As a matter of fact, I have several people that I work with who specialize in doing so. You still need to know about it for yourself so you can maintain that good credit after getting it fixed.

It's almost like the person that goes and gets liposuction, then several months later they are back to their same old self. The reason for that is because although they got the extra weight taken off, they never changed their diets or eating habits. Black America, we first have to renew our minds and not conform to what's going on around us. We have to truly experience transformation in many areas of our lives, especially our finances. That's something that we can control.

We can control how we spend, where we spend, and what we spend our money on. I'm not judging at all. I'm the last person to talk about bad spending habits but, the more I've learned the more adjustments I've had to make. By the way, I'm still learning.

ALT

When I worked as a mortgage lender years ago, I often had to make trips to the State Department and the Pentagon to assist clients with their home loan needs. It wasn't too long after doing so I found myself always stuck in D.C. traffic. I must confess that I cannot stand traffic. So, I finally broke down and purchased my first GPS system. The best thing I liked about my GPS system was that it showed me alternate routes. It didn't make the traffic go away but, the data allowed me to choose another route so I could continue moving towards my destination; that was to get home. My point is that once we have taken control over our mentality and how we see credit, we then need to alter or change our actions.

Is it just me or do you also feel like you're stuck in traffic on the highway of life due to your finances? The light is green but, you can't move because everywhere you look there's congestion. You can feel paralyzed like I did at that airport because of my credit and funds at the time. There's nothing fun about being stuck and held hostage to your financial existence. If what you're doing has gotten you to this place and you're still stuck in traffic, then maybe its time to put aside pride, ego, and comfort and decide to take an alternate route. I can't express to you enough that we have to change or alter our actions if we are to expect different results.

DELETE

I have to be honest with you and say that this is the one thing that has cost me so much money and time; willing to delete bad habits and circles of influences.

My mother really couldn't afford all the latest name brand clothes and shoes for us coming up but, she took pride in making sure that whatever we had was nice and clean. For some reason, that never went over well with my friends in middle school that had on the latest name brand shoes, Jordans.

At times, I was made to feel like I was less than or a nobody because I didn't have on a certain brand. I can laugh now but, I remember one time when my mother bought me two pairs of tennis shoes before school started. They looked just like Jordans from afar but, they were actually called HOOPS. Many of my friends were proud that I had finally made it over to the name-brand family. That was until I was walking down the hallway and my pants leg went up for some reason, and someone yelled, "HOOPS!"

It felt like the whole world came to a halt and all eyes were on me. Thankfully, I was able to press through that moment in life and my personality made way for me. However, within our community we have taken on some bad habits by trying to keep up with the latest name brands. We see it all the time. People will have the newest mobile phone, costing over $1,000, but, fail to get a $15 a month life insurance policy. Or, you'll drive a $40,000 car while renting or living in an apartment instead of owning property. It's important that we delete and get rid of these habits if we are to build wealth.

Now, did I own a Porsche, Mercedes, Eddie Bauer SUV and Nissan Maxima all at once? Yes. I lost them all too. Take it from me, you want to put things in motion that will enable you to have those things when the time is right and when you can pay cash for it.   Sometimes, the people we're around can play a huge part in where we are in life. I never knew that I could have or be more until I got around people that were successful.

Even though it was a struggle for him, my grandfather owned several different businesses at once; teaching me that you should have several streams of income. It was when I was 17- or 18-years old when I was able to associate with people who were financially independent, so I was exposed to it. In many cases, all you need to do is to be around someone that will help you believe that better is possible. A lot of us are around people and in an environment where better doesn't look or seem possible.

Not everyone can just up and leave their environment physically. You may be in a poverty stricken area or on a stressful or meaningless job that you can't leave. You may be incarcerated or live in a negative household with nowhere to go. Many may ask, how do I change my environment to be around successful people? The answer, by reading BOOKS!

You can associate with successful, financially free, wealthy, gifted, spirited, encouraging people through books. Never underestimate the power of words and the associating of them through reading. Remember, earlier I made mention of slaves not being allowed to read? It's extremely hard to hold captive a black man or woman with a book in their hand that they are using. Knowledge makes you powerful but used knowledge makes you a CONQUERER.

Chapter 5

"THIS IS AN ATTEMPT TO COLLECT A DEBT"

I'm already aware that this book will offend some and that it will end up in the hands of people from all different walks of life. So, I wanted to make sure that I wrote something for the lookers in this chapter.

To all of my debt collectors, I know that you're just doing your job and trying to provide for your family so you can too pay off some of your debts and collections, maybe. You're just part of a bigger system that rewards you for collecting money on accounts that your company has decided to invest in. I get that. I know your job is stressful and sometimes you do and say things that you seem forced to do. In many cases you're just picking up bad habits that you've seen other collectors do. No one should have to work under that type of pressure. No one should be forced to be a part of a system that takes advantage of poor people, especially those of the black community. I hope that this book will help you in such a way that you will be inspired to start your own business or a career that's aimed at helping and building people instead of destroying them.

Maybe you're a collector because there were some financial setbacks that had an affect on your credit and hindered you from finding a different career path. Maybe you are working there because you needed a second job to help pay for that house since that lower credit score demands that you pay a higher rate. Or, maybe you love working in collections, your own credit is perfect, you're on the road to creating wealth for you and your family, and you just like harassing people. If so, then this book isn't for you. However, I would still read it because some of the people you're trying to collect on, will walk away from this book feeling differently and will think twice about ever paying another collection again. That's going to have a huge effect on your commissions, by the way.

Okay, now that I have everyone's attention I want to say to those of you that have collection accounts on your credit report I believe that you should NEVER PAY A COLLECTION ACCOUNT AGAIN! Disclaimer, I'm not telling anyone not to pay their debts but, never pay a collection account until the collector can provide you with documentation showing that you've agreed to do business with that collector, which they will not and should not have.

If they haven't written or charged it off, you may owe the creditor not the collectors. So, many collectors have incomplete and inaccurate information that is a violation of your rights as a consumer. If you have harassing collection phone calls or collection accounts affecting your credit, please get to know the FDCPA laws.

The Fair Debt Collections Practice Act governs debt collection practices from abusive, unfair, or deceptive practices which most of them do all three. Calling you all of the time at home and on your job, over and over again is abusive. I'm going to provide you a letter that I've used before to stop the abusive phone calls, just sit tight. Unfair, in my opinion, is when you buy a debt you say I owe from a creditor that has been charged off, then attempt to collect from me for a service I never received from you. How fair is that? Also when they make threats that they are going to take you to court or have you arrested is very deceptive in my opinion.

In many cases, they don't want to go to court because all of the fees aren't worth it; and that's even if they have a license to collect in your state. That's right, many collectors may not even have the right to collect in the state where you reside. Ask them to confirm that they are authorized to collect in your state and see what they come up with.

I've seen people miss out on buying a home, getting a better job, or forced into the arms of predatory lenders for an emergency because of collection accounts and it's so sickening to me. Before I knew better and someone would come to me for a mortgage, I would see some collections on their credit and I would suggest for them to get their collection accounts paid off and try to settle the accounts with the collectors. This was all before I knew better.

The fact of the matter, is that even though you settle with a collector unless you have an agreement in place for them to delete it from your credit report that settled collection account will still weigh negatively on your credit report; like dead weight. If you must pay them because in your heart you feel it's the best thing for you to do, although I disagree, then make sure that you get something in writing that they agree to delete it from all three of your credit reports upon payment. It's called a "Letter of deletion." I would suggest writing a check so that you can have a paper trail and above the endorsement line write, "Agreed to delete from credit reports upon cashing this check." This is only if you feel like you have to pay them.

I know that a lot of what I'm saying in this chapter may be a little bit sketchy to you. You're uncertain because you have been so used to being bullied and told what you had to do by collection agencies and the whole credit system itself. But, trust me I've done these things myself and they work. You can be free from the shackles of collection accounts holding your credit hostage and costing you an abundance of financial upsets and letdowns. You deserve better than what you've been going through.

You may have made some bad decisions in your past or in many cases been misled and made uninformed decisions but, it's not worth a lifetime, or as some would say, seven years of embarrassing moments. I can confirm that there are current laws in place that protect the consumer. If you are educated on some of it you'll have enough ammunition to combat many of these unethical practices. I'll provide one of the letters I used to basically collect from the collectors.

Yes, I said it. I collected from them. What did I collect you ask? I collected my peace of mind back, my time answering calls. I collected my cleaner credit report back and a chance to leverage my credit with getting those items removed. MOVE! Get out the way! So, yes, I basically said to the collectors, "This is an attempt to collect a debt."

Chapter 6

SOME THINGS I THINK YOU SHOULD KNOW

All throughout this book, I'm sharing some of my own experiences and documented historical data that can be researched and found by anyone. I believe that the more you know about a particular subject the better choices one can make when trying to navigate through this whole credit game.

Yes, I called it a game because that's just what it is. Some are winning at this game and there are millions who are losing big time. Black America is coming in last place and is far behind when it comes to this game, however, that no longer has to be the case. If you don't want to be held responsible for where your credit stands and would like to continue to blame someone else after reading this book, then you've wasted your time, money, and have missed the entire purpose of F'D UP MY CREDIT.

I know this game wasn't fair at all when it started but, with all of the knowledge and resources out there now that's available, you can WIN. I need for you to know that where you are doesn't mean that's where you have to stay. I also need for you to know that the rules of the game were never designed for you to win or to be learned but, you can. Understand this, credit can aid in keeping people in bondage or give them an opportunity at freedom. I've met people who were very well-educated and had a six-figure income but, was still a slave to their credit rating. I've had to decline people like that because they didn't have a certain credit score and therefore they had to continue renting and paying higher interest rates on vehicles and credit cards.

On the contrary, I've met people living below the poverty level, on a fixed income, with credit scores in the 700's and 800's with 0% interest on credit cards and little to no debt. This taught me that although income can play a huge part in ones credit health it's not the only major factor. You should know the way you leverage credit and your mindset on how you value it is one of the most important ingredients involved in having a great credit rating.

Another thing you should know, is that the credit bureaus make money off of your information, good or bad. However, the bad credit makes them more. About 90% of lenders use the three major bureaus, Equifax, Experian and TransUnion to get data on you so they can decide if you are a low-risk or high-risk consumer. Based upon how high of a risk you are, they will choose to lend to you at a higher rate or not lend to you at all.

The lenders need this data so they can make an educated- business decision. So, they will pay for a credit report to get that information, sometimes passing that cost on to the customer but, still the bureaus make money from that. Also, once you get an account with that lender they want to report your payment history and other things about the account on you. Guess who they have to pay to receive that reporting and hold that data on you? Yep you guessed it, the credit bureaus.

So, let's say that because that rate was just too high, which made the payments higher for you verses someone else with good credit, you then get behind on your payments and eventually go to collections. The collection agency has purchased your data from the original creditor and begin reporting on you to the credit bureaus again; more money for the credit bureaus when this happens. You might ask, "What does the collection agency have to gain by continuing to report negative items on you and having to pay the bureaus to hold that data?" Well, they feel that if they keep bringing your credit down and you keep getting denied for other items because of that, then eventually you'll pay them. Because you're desperate at that point, you'll be willing to pay the amount, plus fees.

As it relates to your negative credit history, if another creditor decides to allow you to borrow from them, they'll gladly charge you a much higher rate. That makes them more money than someone with a good credit rating anyway.

As you can see, your bad credit is a money-maker for several businesses and you're the one that suffers. It's no wonder the credit bureaus aren't eager to remove negative items off of your credit report, whether the negative item is yours or not. That's why agencies like the CFPB and acts like the FCRA had to step in and put laws in place to protect the consumer. The sad part is that many have no clue of their rights, especially in the black community.

Something else you should know is that discrimination within the financial sector has been going on for years. It is still happening even now. I'll show you a little later some of the big financial institutions I'm sure you have had or still have accounts with them today that were found guilty of such acts. For protection purposes, I won't exactly list them by their corporate names. You'll have to use your mind to guess based upon the clues I give you.

In addition to financial institutions, just recently there have been acts of discrimination when it comes to housing and credit by those that choose to market via social media. Many won't see this unless they use and buy Facebook Ads but, now they have a guideline that you must attest to and agree with that speaks about not using that marketing platform to discriminate against certain ethnicities or groups of people.

There were many complaints of these acts and it was discovered that when it came to employment, housing information, and credit offers that those paying for marketing ads were excluding blacks and hispanics from seeing these ads. On Facebook's it states the following, "While we are asking all advertisers to review and accept our non-discrimination policy, it's especially important for advertisers running housing, employment and credit ads." This is a clear indication that there's still an effort right here in the land of the free and the home of the brave to exclude and withhold information from minority groups, especially blacks as it relates to employment, housing and credit; all of which are vitally important when it comes to making a living, and attempting to create wealth to pass on to the next generation.

As I expressed earlier, I wanted you to be in the know about some of the financial institutions that were caught discriminating. I want you to know that there's a reason that some will do anything so that you don't have a chance at winning in this financial game. They know that once you get closer to gaining your financial freedom then they will be less likely to control you. A black man or woman that's free physically, mentally, spiritually, and financially is a threat.

So let's take a small break from all this heavy stuff and play a match game. Here's how it's going to go. I'm going to list some clues of different financial institutions that were discovered discriminating and then I'll also list the incident as well as the law suit, then let's see if you can match them up correctly. Here we go:

1. Hells Fargo

2. Sun DisTrust

3. Jank of America

4. Walk-Ova-Ya

5. Chase you Down

6. Capital None

***

Write the number of the bank in the lines below above the cases or write the name in the allotted spaces within the law suit description.

_____

The suit, filed last Friday, in the U.S. District Court for the Eastern District of California, accuses (   ) of targeting African-American and Latino communities in Sacramento for issuing loans with more expensive and higher risk compared to loans made to white borrowers. The complaint accused (   ) of practicing discrimination against minority borrowers for more than a decade with the aim of recording higher earnings.

_____

The National Association for the Advancement of Colored People, Houston Branch ("NAACP"), League of United Latin American Citizens, District VIII ("LULAC") and a former bank employee have filed a major federal racial discrimination lawsuit. The three parties allege that ( ) has made a deliberate plan to close banks in Black and Latino communities while keeping banks in white communities.

———

The suit claimed that the ( ) practiced "uniform and national in scope" discrimination against African-American financial advisors, such as assigning them to poorer bank branches, understaffing them, and failing to include them in a program for richer clients.

———

( ) was ordered Monday to pay 1,147 African American job applicants $2,181,593 in back wages and interest after a judge found that the company's Charlotte office had racially discriminated against them.

———

(   ) will pay $21 million to settle a

federal lawsuit alleging the company charged black and

Hispanic borrowers more than others for loans, according to

papers filed Thursday with the Richmond U.S. District Court.

***This one is a Bonus. Although not related to race, still
discrimination that resulted in a law suit by a group that still
today, have to fight against an unfair system.***

———————

(   ) has agreed to pay $5.5 million

to settle allegations by the U.S. Department of Labor that it

engaged in compensation discrimination against 2,021

current and former female employees over six years.

There are many more cases that can be

researched and reveal where big financial institutions have

been involved with acts of discrimination against blacks here

in America. I can honestly say that some of them have efforts

in place to right their wrongs and offer services to people and communities that have been disenfranchised, left out, or left behind in many financial wealth-building opportunities. I'll leave out that those institutions in some cases benefit financially from the government when they offer those types of programs and sometimes will pay their loan consultants extra bonuses for booking those types of loans. Ya'll didn't hear that from me. Still, I commend them for recognizing and offering something. It's a start.

It's been said that, "Education is the Great Equalizer," and I believe that we accept "No" because of what we don't "Know". Once we desire education, knowledge, and wisdom more than acceptance, and a Popeye's chicken sandwich, we can then begin leveling the playing field and creating our own opportunities.

Please don't confuse degrees, universities, and college with education. I commend anyone that has done all of what I just mentioned. I've even done so myself with a Bachelors,

Masters, and now gearing up for pursuing a Doctoral degree. However, the knowledge and education I'm speaking of is something that's learned from experience, even if it's someone else's experience.

Black America has to get better at putting ourselves in a position to learn from others who have done what we desire to do. Then we must be willing to teach others in our community to duplicate those efforts. Thanks to the internet, I believe the knowledge is out there for the taking. We just have to want it bad enough which is a mindset change, a renewing of the mind. The bible says, "Be ye, transformed by the renewing of your mind..." We have to start thinking and knowing that we belong. We are better than just making it from paycheck to paycheck. We are meant for success. We are APPROVED! Just something I thought you should know.

Chapter 7

YOU'RE APPROVED

With over 15-years of working in the mortgage lending industry, one of the best feelings in the world is being able to call a customer back and tell them maybe the best news of their day and that's, "YOU'RE APPROVED."

A large percentage of people these days have some insight on whether or not they will be approved for a loan then there's some that have no idea. The real question is, what are you approved for? Did you get approved for a mortgage with a smaller loan amount, limiting what area of town you can raise your kids in? Or, is it the car loan that you were approved for but, the interest rate is double what was advertised in bold on the"you're approved" mailer with the life-like key attached to it? Could it be that you were approved for that credit card finally with a $300 credit limit, $99 annual fee, 15% to 26% interest rate?

Many lenders started to realize that denying too many people would put them out of business. The people with good credit have options and end up paying very small interest rates as opposed to those with fair and poor credit. Therefore, lenders had to create products for those with not-so-desirable credit so they could pay the higher rates and fees to make up for the loss or slow profits they were making from the good or great credit clients. Due to the fact that those that didn't have the best credit weren't attractive to most lenders, by telling them "You're Approved" would make them feel appreciated and willing to accept just about whatever terms were thrown their way.

It's like there being someone that no one wants to date and them feeling that everyone thinks that they aren't attractive. Then, all of a sudden someone comes along and tells them that they are beautiful and wanted. That unwanted person, once they get over the fact that someone told them what they never thought they would hear, unfortunately, will begin to accept any terms or treatment from that one who so-called gave them a chance. They are willing to stay in that relationship all the way until they get used up and find themselves in a worse situation than before.

Believe it or not, lenders will play that same game over and over again until they've made that person with fair credit get to poor credit, and they've gained profit from that high interest rate. Just like that person in my earlier example, nothing will change until you discover the value in yourself and take advantage of the resources and examples all around you.

I've been blessed to see all types of credit reports and how people manage their credit. My heart goes out to people that are flying and navigating in the dark. The sad part, is that it wasn't until recently when I began to see the value in leveraging credit and that me and my family deserved to be a player in this game to win.

Despite what mistakes you've made and what you've done with your credit, you still deserve to win. I will not accept that it's all your fault and that a system designed to work against you shouldn't be called out and held partly responsible. Despite how you've been made to feel, you do belong and you are meant for greatness. Do the necessary work and expect approvals, not because it was given but because you earned it. Also, not just any approval but approvals that will put you and your family in a better state. We have to get to a point where we stop excepting the scraps and the traps that have been laid before us but, be observant and ask more and more questions.

By now, you should've gotten something from the words within this book to at least have you thinking differently and be inspired to seek out, learn, and put into action some methods that can be life-changing. If that's not the case, then thank you for the donation and please drop my book off at your local Goodwill store, so it can be on sale for $2.00 next to a 1983 romance novel.

For those or you that have gotten something from this book and not just a tax write off, then allow "You're Approved" to be added to your daily affirmations to yourself. You have to approve you before anyone else will. The more and more you begin to tell yourself that, your mind will begin to open up and attract ways to align you with that which you speak. Stop saying what you don't have and how unfair it all seems. Consistently repeating 5 + 5 will never solve for the answer without including the = sign. You have to involve the equal, which gives way to solving the problem.

It's nothing wrong with acknowledging the problem but you can't sit there and dwell on it and then complain and blame others for not solving it. Oh, five plus five equals ten by the way because I know your mind was still pondering on that. Do you see how your mind automatically wants to go into problem-solving mode? However, we have a bad habit of putting up obstacles and roadblocks in our own way.

Once you renew your mind and put some action behind what you've learned I want you to be able to walk into any bank and confidently say, "I already know that I'm approved, I just need to see what I'm approved for because here's what I'll accept."

There's only a few slight adjustments and a bit of time that's in-between now and you being able to do that. The knowledge is available, right now and the credit rating system is still regulated by laws that protect the consumer, you just have to be exposed to it and run with what you've learned. I've mentioned a few methods that I've tried and it has helped me. I've listed several contacts and resources of people's work that I've seen and tried their techniques and they work. I would suggest that you have a selection of books and videos on credit. No one has all the answers but, there's a lot of great information out there to help you get in a position of consistently hearing, "You're Approved!"

Chapter 8

NOT MUCH TO DO WITH CREDIT

Please don't be alarmed or too disappointed by this chapter. I wanted to take a break from this whole credit stuff per se, and talk about several other different issues that are on my mind.

When my wife and I were writing, producing, and acting in our own stage plays one of the things I would love to do is go off-script. The audience would love it and it would be fun to me to see the cast improv with me and even laugh on stage at times. I know some of the high-class, professional stage play producers would find going off-script unprofessional. But, in your production you can do what you want to do. Same here. When you write your book, do as you please but, this is mine so I'll do the same and go off-script.

I'm writing this book at a very interesting time here in America because it's Presidential Campaigning season. The promises and tension are at an all-time lie. Wait, I meant to say all-time high. One of the topics being talked about is Reparations for African Americans here in the Unites States that were descendants of slaves.

While in some cases America feels as if she has apologized for the wrong-doings of slavery and other horrible eras, many blacks feel as if that apology, with little-to-no action, is just words. The main reason behind slavery was to create and generate wealth. So, why not repay back in that same way?

It's almost like buying something that cost two dollars. You give them a one hundred dollar bill and they give you your change back in coupons to shop in their store. Would you go for that? Hel... I mean Heck Naw! You want what's owed to you back in cash.

If, and that's a big IF, reparations are given, in my opinion, they need to do several things. It should hit the wealthiest country in the world in the pockets. Yes, it needs to cost America financially. Also, reparations should assist in repairing so many unfair systems that slavery caused by making efforts in several areas.

Just imagine if every African American with a valid ID were given $50,000-$100,000, a $2000 a-month housing voucher for 5-7 years, a fresh start with an 800-credit score, eliminate all student-loan debt, and all negative items reported to the bureaus from that credit report were removed. One more thing. For all of those in prison on non-violent offenses and that worked; when they get out give them back-pay for all or most of the hours worked at the current minimum-wage rate. Also make those companies that they worked for while in prison, hire them if they need employment. Private prisons would surely vanish or change from what we know them to be now. How would this change your financial status? Would life be different if you had this type of relief? I know for my family and I it would.

I made mention of prison and I'd like to speak some more on that for a moment. We have seen time after time where the justice system we have here in America has a long record of being unjust for African Americans. All of us I'm sure know someone that's in or has been to prison for non-violent crimes. We also know that our country has a history of giving longer sentences to blacks than they do to whites for the exact same crime.

Many would say that if they do the crime then they should do the time and for the most part I agree with that. But, it should be universal no matter what color you are or what your economic status is. There are black and poor people right now spending time behind bars for selling marijuana with the same sentence as someone that has murdered someone. In my opinion, that's an unjust justice system. I'm just saying.

The crazy part, is that the same marijuana that they were locked up for is now becoming legal across the country. The government has now found a way to tax it and make profits from it. By the way, I never understood how a plant that grows out of the ground was made illegal for you to consume it. I do get the false efforts of the "War on Drugs." (That was really a war on African Americans and poor people). Also, when blacks were addicted to crack it was a crime and they were placed in prison. But, when whites became addicted to opioids it was an epidemic and was said that they needed professional help. Don't trip, I'm just going off-script still.

I have a lot more to say but, I'll just mention one more thing. I'm hoping that this part won't offend my church folks, yet encourage and inspire a shift in focus when it comes to finances, especially in the "black churches."

While I don't believe that the church is or should be a color as opposed to just being a body or family of believers, we all know the truth that in our society there is a such thing as black and white churches. Sunday morning is one of the most divided and segregated days here in America. As it relates to black churches and equipping the body with financial knowledge there is a lot left to be desired.

There's a strong effort for members to sow and they are taught that GOD will give them the increase. While I believe that GOD will provide, I also feel like HE wants us to manage our resources in a way that's not keeping us in bondage. I've known people that gave the last of their bill money to the church and ended up in the dark. Or some who have taken out home-equity loans to meet their financial pledge to the church for a building fund and end up defaulting on the loan. I understand that when we give it should be a from-the-heart sacrifice but, at the same time the church should operate in the same manner.

Members are asked to sow in faith but, when in need in many cases, the church won't do the same. Truth be told, in the bible days if a member was in need the body assisted with that need so no one went without. Today, we have many going without and a select few going with an abundance. I won't go into a bashing of Pastors that are doing well financially. I don't see anything wrong with that as long as they are willing to empower their members to find their purpose and help them prosper as well.

I know a lot of Pastors that endure pain, time spent away from their own families, and even huge financial burdens that most members will never have to experience. I also know some that take on burdens that were never designed for them to take on. As a whole, the family of GOD must do better for all and not just a small few. We can't keep trying to convince people that the more they put in the offering plate the more their finances will improve.

In many cases, I've seen people in the same or worse situations behind doing that without being equipped and educated on how to create, manage, and invest their finances. I'm not being biased or anything but, churches need to have on-going educational trainings on credit and how to leverage it. If people can get out of financial bondage they'd be more willing and able to give towards the ministry.

Also, there needs to be more education within the "black churches" on life insurance. Now, I know that's something we don't like talking about and that's planning for ourselves or one of our loved ones dying but, that's the reality of it. We have to get to a point where we understand the value and the benefit of life insurance. Other races have used this for years to help build wealth and give their children a good head start financially.

Think about it. What if the church developed a plan that allowed its members to pay into it as a group? They could purchase huge insurance policies for those that choose to participate. Just a thought. I'm done going off for now, so back to your regularly scheduled program.

Chapter 9

FROM DOING SEASON TO DUE SEASON

One of my mentors, is a minister from my hometown of Houston, Texas.Tim Daniels, taught me that there was a fifth season. Of course, most of us were taught about the four seasons; Winter, Spring, Summer, and Fall. So, as he was teaching about this fifth one in one of his sermons, I was zoned in on how someone so articulate and well-educated could make the mistake of assuming and teaching that there were five seasons.

As the lesson unfolded, my eyes were opened to a new perspective on life. See, at that point I didn't know that I would have to bury my son, grandmother, father, brother, cousin, mother, and another grandmother all within a six-year period. I remember one time talking to him on the phone after letting him know that my grandmother died and how it seemed like all of my family that I grew up knowing were dying off. He said something that took me back to when I heard him preach that sermon regarding the seasons. He said, that I was just "going through a season."

In that lesson he taught a couple of years prior, that fifth season he spoke about was what he called "Due Season." Galatians 6:9 says, "And let us not be weary in well DOING: for in DUE season we shall reap, if we faint not." Now, I'll be honest with you and say that I'm not even going to try and articulate how and what all he shared in that lesson. I actually don't remember it all. But, those of you that believe in GOD and have faith know what I mean when I say, "It spoke to my spirit."

Therefore, I'll tie that into credit and how we need to get doing so that we can partake in our due season. First, I want to talk about the four seasons that most of us are familiar with and can relate to.

Winter. I look at it as a time in my life when I was out of the eagle's nest. I had just finished high school and was off to college at Texas Tech University into what some would call a "cold world." I was about eight hours away from home and in a place where I had to figure some things out for myself. With so many feelings of uncertainty and ignorant to managing money, I was a prime candidate to being taken advantage of by any creditor. After all, I had never been taught about the importance of credit and how credit is used.

As I mentioned before, at a very early age I was exposed to wealthy people and entrepreneurs from different walks of life through a multi-level marketing company that I was involved in. Yet, I still knew nothing about leveraging credit. Truth be told, in the business that I was in paying for things with cash was highly praised. It was a very cold world for me as a young man.

Spring. This was where the real illusion began. For me, it was an eye- opening experience. Just like the spring, it felt good that someone was willing to give me this little plastic card with money on it that I could use and didn't have to payback all at once.

Remember that time when you got your first credit card? Maybe you were like me, in college trying to budget whatever money you had just to make it from week to week. Then all of a sudden, there was someone at this little table in the student center running a credit promotion that seemed too good to refuse. You filled out the form and signed the dotted line and not too long after that, you get your first credit card in the mail with a $1000 credit limit.

Summer. You look up and before you know it, you're

buying summa this and summa that; taking your friends out to eat, buying things you don't need and not really caring about the price. In my case, I bought a plane ticket to visit my home in Houston. It felt so good to be able to buy things without worrying about the price. I was finally looking like some of those business people I had been around. With little to no worry, all I had to do when I got to the register was pull out my new credit card. "Thank you for your purchase, Mr. Roberts."

I was 18-years old and I felt on top of the world; water tasted wetter, food tasted better, my clothes seemed to fit just right. Shoot, it even seemed like the sun was shinning a little bit brighter. That was until I got back to school and tried to make a purchase and, "I'm sorry, Mr. Roberts. Your card has been declined."

My Summer season ended quicker than I had expected and it seemed like my newborn credit history was beginning to fall apart.

Fall. Fall seemed to be one that took a long time climbing out of. Have you ever been at a point in life where it all seems to be falling apart? Things look as if you can't win for losing. You take two steps forward and life knocks you three steps back. You have to live from paycheck to paycheck. You have less money than you do month. I had never felt so rejected in my life up to that point when my credit card got declined.

It seemed as if I had just got the card. I knew I didn't spend $1000 that fast. So, like any other responsible young adult, guess what I did? Yep, you're right. I applied and got another credit card. I was back to living my best life, catching flights, buying any meals I wanted to, and eventually maxing out another card.

Suddenly, I started getting bills in the mail and at the time they'd seem small; until I missed the due date. I then learned a lesson on interest charges real fast. Before I knew it, I started making late payments and having missed payments. This led to charge-offs and collections. I also learned how to screen calls and disguise my voice to avoid some of those collection calls. Like so many others, I fell hard and for a long time.

My finances were a mess. At the time, I was working as a bank teller at the bank across from my school's campus. I didn't have control over my own finances yet I was handling other people's money; check out the irony in that.

Everyday, I walked into to work; literally because I didn't own a car at the time. I would come into work everyday feeling so hypocritical. This was no way for a young, college student to live and try to focus on getting decent grades. It's no wonder why I had a few failing grades. Okay, not really. Most days, I didn't feel like going to class plus, I was busy working.

I had my own soap distribution business, was working at the athletic dining hall on campus, all while working as a bank teller. I didn't have a problem working hard and brining in money. I started working at the age of thirteen at my grandfather's construction business that was attached to his barbershop that was attached to his cafe'. So, I was no stranger to work.

I remember one time in college my mom called me and was a little concerned because I hadn't called her for any money in a while. That's because I had money coming in but, still never understood that credit was more even powerful than money. I know that's a bold statement but, I've seen more people buy homes with no money if they had the credit verses the other way around. Credit is a powerful resource that should be valued and understood on how it works. Y'all ready for the other season I learned about?

DUE season. Many times, we'll get excited and shout when we hear the part "for in due season we shall reap" and oftentimes forget the first part of that very same verse. It says,

"Let us not grow weary in well doing..." That tells me that we have to *do* to get to the due.

We have to put in some work sowing before we can reap. One of the major issues is that due to lack of knowledge there are many who are in the black community that have no clue as to what to do, especially when it comes to utilizing credit to our advantage. I promise you that I'm not trying to preach you a sermon but, for me in many cases, my faith was all I had. Acts 7:30 says, "God used to wink at ignorance but now commands all, everywhere to repent." Repentance is a change of mind that will lead to a change of action. In order for us to really advance within this credit system game that's being played we have to do at least four things to get on track.

1. Renew or reset our thought process - Cease from thinking that things are just the way they are. You were meant for greatness and many people have made some of the same financial mistakes we've made but, they got out of their

situation because they knew the game.

2. Get the knowledge - Read, research, and listen to people with a proven success record when it comes to building or rebuilding credit. I find it interesting that there are so many credit repair companies out there. Some of them are really good but, there are others just once again praying on the poor and desperate.

3. Use the knowledge we get - Yes, knowledge is power. But, used-knowledge is more powerful. Once you learn how to rebuild your credit then use that knowledge to your advantage and pass it on!

4. Stay committed to the process by delayed gratification - We have to be willing to forgo having the latest name brands or buying a car with a high interest rate so we can look like we're successful to the outside world. I know why we do that though. Kanye said it best, "They made us hate ourselves and love their wealth." Deny yourself now as you go through the

process of rebuilding your credit.

You may be asking, "How do I rebuild my credit?" Here's my disclaimer, I'm not a credit repair guru. I didn't write this book to fix your credit but, I wrote this book to fix your mindset on how you value it. I will however give some of my contacts that I used to FIX UP MY CREDIT.

They are experts and have a wealth of knowledge that they give away for free in addition to some of the services they are compensated for. I'm not going to just leave you with that though, I do want to give you some sample letters I used to assist me with my journey to repairing my own credit that I think may be helpful to you. Hey what do you have to lose, right?

*****SENT VIA CERTIFIED MAIL*****

Letter to the credit bureaus:

* * *

Date

Name

Address

City, State, Zip

SSN:

DOB:

CREDIT BUREAU NAME

CREDIT BUREAU ADDRESS

This correspondence is being written to request verifiable proof (an original signed contract with my signature on it) kept on record with your company. In an environment where fraudulent activity and identity theft is at an all time high, verifiable proof is a must. Also according to Section 609 in the Fair Credit Reporting Act (FCRA), upon request you must "clearly and accurately disclose" the requested information to the consumer. I am not requesting a screenshot, statement printout or transaction history. These items aren't considered valid or verifiable proof. This would mean that any company could send in a statement from anywhere to you and your company would report it without having proof that the account belongs to a particular consumer.

If there's any account that you deem as valid and verified, I am also requesting for you to provide me with the process you used to conduct your investigation. I will expect to receive a copy of the original creditors documentation that you keep on file.

* * *

Under, Section 611 (5)(A) of the FCRA – it requires you to "…
DELETE all information which cannot be verified within 30
days." I am also aware of the Civil liability and the remedy
available to me. Section 617 (Civil liability for negligent
noncompliance) states:

(a) In general. Any person who is negligent in failing to
comply with any requirement imposed under this title with
respect to any consumer is liable to that consumer in an
amount equal to the sum of:

(1) any actual damages sustained by the consumer as a
result of the failure; and

(2) in the case of any successful action to enforce any
liability under this section, the costs of the action together

with reasonable attorney's fees as determined by the court.

I'm expecting for the following accounts be verified or removed immediately promptly.

Account	Account Number	Physical Verification
0000000	1234567891011	Unverified Account

* Please remove all non-account holding inquiries over 30 days old.

* * *

* Please add a Promotional Suppression to my credit file.

Thank You,

Jeremie Roberts

IN WITNESS WHEREOF, the said party has signed and sealed these presents the day and year first above written.

Signed, sealed and delivered in the presence of:

_____

STATE OF

COUNTY OF

I HEREBY CERTIFY that on this day before me, an officer duly qualified to take acknowledgments, personally appeared

_____ who has produced _____ as identification and who executed the foregoing instrument and he/ she acknowledged before me that he/ she executed the same.

WITNESS my hand and official seal in the County and State aforesaid this _____ day of _____ 2019.

* * *

Notary Public

Printed Name

My commission expires:

This letter is to the collection agency so they can leave you alone and stop calling you titled, "Say Bruh stop calling my phone." Okay, not really. Below is what you can use:

*****SENT VIA CERTIFIED MAIL*****

* * *

Creditor

City, State, Zip

RE: REQUEST FOR CEASING PHONE CALLS

Dear [name]:

The ongoing and repetitive phone calls made by your company to me concerning account #12345670, has been very disturbing and can be seen as abusive. I'm conducting an investigation regarding this account you claim belongs to me and until this account can be verified and validated, I can not pay on this bill.

According to **15 USCA 1692 c of the Fair Debt Collection**

Practices Act, this serves as my notice for you to cease all telephone calls unless permitted by federal law. I am not ceasing communication with your company but requesting for all communication to me be in writing.

Sincerely,

YOUR FULL NAME

Address

City, State, Zip

These are just a couple items that can assist with getting your scores up and minimize the harassing phone calls while you try to focus on working through this process. Thanks to technology, we have unlimited information at our fingertips to advance us to our due season, we just have to do the work.

I'm not sure about you but, I'm tired of just getting by, wishing and hoping for better for me and my family. I wish it hadn't taken me so long to realize how credit played a vital role in financial freedom. Have you even imagined a life where finances weren't an issue? You didn't have to depend on a paycheck to fund your bills and dreams at the same time. Take it from me, if you cannot relate it just doesn't feel good at all.

There were times when I would go to the store and when I got to the register I already had an excuse in mind to verbalize just in case my card didn't go through. "You know what? I deactivated that card. I totally forgot. Let me run to the car and get my other one." That's no way for a grown man to live, especially when the item was under ten dollars.

Of course, something that we as blacks here in America know how to do is fake it 'til we hopefully make it; and fake the making it part too. This can be a stressful cycle. We've mastered the art of pretending and acting like everything is okay when it's not. I will say that we got it honestly.

See, many of our ancestors had to pretend to be something they weren't just to survive, while knowing deep down that something just wasn't right. On the other hand, there were many that fought and died making a statement to those that had them enslaved and that was "enough is enough." That did that knowing that death could or would be in their near future.

Are you willing to die to the old way of how you've been doing things for the possibility of freedom? Just know that if you are there's a strong chance you'll get labeled by those that wish to keep you in bondage and in many cases discouraging actions and words from some of the closest people to you as well. Don't get weary in well-doing, remember? Keep doing the work. Yes, it will take discipline and consistency but know that freedom isn't free and being in financial bondage isn't either. Just ask someone paying a high interest rate. Being broke is expensive. Take it from me.

Here are some of the contacts I promised you. They all were instrumental in educating me and assisting me one way or another with Fixing Up My Credit.

Credit Repair and Real Estate Investment Services

Jay Morrison

844-564-6562

booking@mrjaymorrison.com

www.jaymorrisonacademy.com

Neko Cheri

www.nekocheri.com

Corey P. Smith

www.coreypsmith.com

Books: Conspiracy of Credit, Outsmart the Credit Bureaus,

Unbreakable Laws of Business Credit

Life Insurances Services:

Ivan & Stephanie Wilson (The Wilson-Group-NAA)

252-379-5975

Financial Advisor:

Dr. Marcus Barnum

VP of Investments and Financial Advisor

www.marcusbarnum.com

drmarkbarnum@gmail.com

713-201-2417

Conclusion

I've come to learn that the credit reporting system just like many other systems here in America isn't broken but, more so it was constructed that way. Most of the unfair treatment due to race and ethnicity is operating as expected but, shouldn't be accepted.

It wasn't expected for blacks here in America to be treated equally and to be just as wealthy as whites along with equal pay for work. Nor were there any expectations of blacks being a free and un-oppressed people. Slavery wasn't designed to end. On the surface it may be but, the remodeled and upgraded form of it still exists today; not just for blacks but for the poor as well.

When there's oppression there's suppression and when there's suppression there's depression. It's no wonder why so many of us are depressed. The sad part is that eight out of ten of us are living with some form of depression and six out of the eight don't even know it.

Please forgive the plug here but, my wife has a book coming out called *Naked Truth: A Christian's Battle With Anxiety And Depression*. See, in the black community we've been conditioned to look at depression and getting professional help for that as an embarrassment to us and our family, also as a sign of weakness. This has been going on for generations; never addressing this important issue. What we don't handle gets handed down to our children and it keeps going.

Although it can seem that there's no light at the end of

the tunnel for Black America, I believe that we have so many things working for us and our good compared to what our ancestors had. There are doors of opportunities that our grandparents and their parents didn't have. We, because of them, can open and walk through the door and make a way. We have to take a deep hard look into who we are and what's inside each and every one of us.

Think about this. If that one ancestor of yours didn't live through all of the pain and struggle then you wouldn't be here today. You are built up of the most powerful and resilient DNA in the world. Out of the people during the slave trade many were killed, jumped or thrown overboard, died in transit due to different illnesses, dehydration, hunger, and many other things. Someone in your ancestry made it here. They made it here and so now you, we, can tap into that enduring power to press on. Shame on us if we don't take and make something better of ourselves for our children's, children's, children. This is what's inside of us and who we are. No amount of bondage, debt, or placed limitations should be able to change that.

My wife and kids convinced me to buy a dog. Before we picked the dog up, my wife had already connected with that dog online and she already had a name for him. Get this y'all, she named him Cinnamon. Yep. A male named, Cinnamon. I told her that there's no males that go by the name Cinnamon unless he's a stripper, right?

Okay. I digress from what I was saying. So, dogs have this thing inside of them where they bark. That's who they are and that's what they do. What I've noticed is that whether he's in his crate or he's running free, he still barks. Even with his leash on and the distance that he can travel is limited, he still barks. Cinnamon can be in the dark or with all of the lights on, he still barks. He's going to be what GOD has put on the inside of him to be no matter if he's in a crate, on a leash, in the dark, in the light, or roaming free.

What am I saying? No matter if we are in a cage, in a dark chapter of our lives, have limited resources, or if the sun is shining down on us, we need to discover meaning to uncover the greatness that's already inside of us. Everyday I'm learning that it's there and the knowledge to develop what's on the inside of us is out there and at our fingertips.

My mom used to have a saying and it took me becoming an adult to really understand what she was saying. She would say, "The rich keeps getting richer and the poor keeps getting poorer." This has to change and used knowledge and education along with determination, can be the great equalizer.

It hurts saying this but, our ignorance plays a huge part in us staying where we are and in bondage. Where we are isn't all our fault but, where we stay is. Being a black man here in America is the only angle I can truly speak from, so excuse me if I've offended anyone but, my truth is my truth. Of course I've made many mistakes and I'm sure as long as I keep living I will make many more.

I'm okay with that. What I'm not okay with is standing on the sidelines watching our history being rewritten and we're still in the same place mentally we were hundreds of years ago.

My mother tried hard to keep me out of a system that was designed as a trap for a black man. As I'm writing this book now in 2019 there's a Netflix series called "When They See Us." It's giving so much insight and is uncovering the truths and pulling back the curtains on a justice system that wrongfully trapped five boys that were locked up for a crime that they didn't commit back in 1986. Thank GOD they've been fully exonerated but, I mention this for two reasons.

One, I hope and pray that you'll have the time to see it. Second, because like so many other young, black boys in

America that could've been me. I remember a friend of mine driving at the age of sixteen. I was about fourteen or fifteen and there were several times we would get pulled over by the cops because they would see two black boys riding in a Lincoln Continental with bass in the trunk. That's loud music by the way just in case some of y'all don't get it. One time, they made us get out and place our hands on the car while they looked in there. God must have heard my mother's prayers, because they would always let us go.

Another time, two cops were standing outside a convenient store as I exited gripping a brown paper bag with one hand. My mother was sitting in the car waiting for me. One of the cops said, "Hey, I bet you're used to carrying bags like that." Granted, I wasn't as fearful as one would expect, being about thirteen. Besides my ride or die was out there. I replied, "No, Sir. This is how I carry my trophies and awards."

I continued walking and got in the car. Of course my mom asked me what he had said to me. I told her what he said and my reply. She was so proud at that moment but, I could still see the worry in her eyes, wondering what will the future in this country hold for her baby boy.

I want to thank each and every one of you for taking the time to read this book. Also, please forgive me for taking so long to write this information down. Honestly, I should've written this book ten years ago but, life had to unfold giving me more content to write.

Sometimes it takes losing everything to realize that GOD has given you something deep down inside that can't be taken. My prayer is that there's a change to this whole credit rating system to making it more of an equal starting point than where we are now. I know some may feel that it's already equal but, for Black America there wasn't a head start, nor insight into the rules of the game when it first started. So, yes, in 2019 we're still playing catch-up.

Is it possible? I believe it is. I believe that we're in an age where we can take unequal opportunities and become equal as it relates to financial health. I didn't write this book to tear any particular race down but, I wanted to speak to my race; to help lift someone up.

Please don't label me as an "ist" just because I want to tell my race of people that have been told the opposite for so long, that Black is Beautiful; Black is Powerful; Black is Gifted; Black is Intelligent; Black is Strong; Black is Love; Black is Unity; Black is Excellence; Black is Happiness; Black is Black.

In the beginning of this book I told a story about a life changing experience and I know that some of you may be wondering if I ever got a chance to see my mother in the hospital that day. YES! I was able to see her, hug her, kiss her, and spend as much time with her as I was allowed. Time went by and eventually mom passed away from cancer. Although having to sit there and wait for my mother to pass away was one of the most hurtful experiences in my life, I was still able to see how GOD was there with us every step of the way. Just know, that no matter where you are in life right now you are not "a loan". Okay, I had to just because of the type of book this is. My bad. God loves you, I love you and you are not alone!

About The Author

Jeremi'e G. Roberts is a mortgage consultant and entrepreneur who has generated millions of dollars for one of the largest financial institutions in the world. With over a decade of analyzing credit and assisting a wide range of clients with homeownership, Jeremi'e has developed a need and a passion for educating the uninformed of the value of credit.

Acknowledgements

First I'd like to start off by saying that GOD has blessed me more than I could even imagine. I'm not worthy of HIS love and grace. Time and time again HE reveals HIMSELF to me in some of the most simple ways. I'm so thankful that HE never gives me what I deserve. THANK YOU for always giving me another chance to serve you by serving others.

This book wouldn't have even been possible or a thought in my mind had it not been for my super-intelligent and gorgeous wife. It was her idea to write a book of her own and I only entertained the idea to encourage her along the way. All of a sudden I learned that all of us have a book within us based upon our own experiences in life. You have always been my most loyal and honest supporter. You make me better even when it means laying aside and putting your dreams and goals on hold. Thank you for loving me, loving our children, and for teaching me more about me.

A few other people I'd like to mention who were all inspirations to me throughout this journey. Leonard Chatman Jr, thank you for trusting me with your vision and brand. I never knew that while I was designing your book cover, advising you and riding with you on your journey, that I would also be a student of the great work that you are doing. Jackie and JP, thanks for always being an encouragement and supporting everything I do. Wanda, Katandra, Joanne, Calvin, and Cayla, thank you for trusting me enough to take some of my credit advice. Cayla, while I was writing this part, I was also on the phone with you while you got approved for your first credit card. How cool is that! To all of my Brothers of Kappa Alpha Psi, Inc., thank you for believing in me and for always pushing me to achieve in all that I do. Thank you, to my Roberts family, Mock family, and Waller family for always loving me the way you do. To all of my church families all over the country and in different parts of the world, thank you for embracing me and my different self.

All of my clients, thank you for believing enough in me to be a part of your dream and allowing me to play a small role in making it a reality for you and your family. Brandon, Derrika, Neko, Jay, and Corey, you all have impacted me and have played a major part in waking me up to something that I should've paid more attention to years ago. You guys are the best at what you do and just know that you're changing the lives of people, that will change the lives of other people, that will change lives. This is a much needed movement in our community and I'm just thankful to have the confidence to share what I know with others.

Lastly, to all of my children, thank you for being willing to share your dad with so many other people. I know you have sacrificed time with me so that I could share whatever gifts I may have with others. Just know that GOD will reward you for your love, long suffering, and patience with me. You are my greatest gifts.

RESOURCES

Dr. Martin Luther King's Economics: Through Jobs, Freedom Mark Engler - https://www.thenation.com/article/dr-martin-luther- kings-economics-through-jobs-freedom/

Bank Of America Ordered To Pay $2.2 Million To 1,000 Black Job Seekers It Discriminated Against David Knowles - https://www.nydailynews.com/news/national/bank-america-discriminated-blacks-pay-2-2-million-article-1.1465391

Wells Fargo Advisors To Pay $35.5 Million To Settle Race Discrimination Suit https://advisorhub.com/wells-fargo-advisors- pay-35-5-million-settle-race-discrimination-suit/

Jpmorgan Pays $55m To Settle Mortgage Discrimination Lawsuit Nathan Bomey - https://www.usatoday.com/story/money/ 2017/01/18/us-accuses-jpmorgan-mortgage-discrimination-lawsuit/96710486/

Naacp Files Racial Discrimination Lawsuit Against Capital One Bank Adedamola Agboola - https://www.blackenterprise.com/naacp- racial-lawsuit-capital-one-bank/

Justice Department Reaches $21 Million Settlement To Resolve Allegations Of Lending Discrimination By Suntrust Mortgage https://www.justice.gov/opa/pr/ justice-department-reaches-21- million-settlement-resolve-allegations-lending-discrimination

Wells Fargo, Wachovia Gender Discrimination Class Action Settlement
Sarah Mirando - https://topclassactions.com/lawsuit-settlements/ lawsuit-news/1049-wells-fargo-wachovia-gender-discrimination- class-action-settlement/

Made in the USA
Middletown, DE
06 January 2020